Runaway Train

Saved by Belle of the Mines and Mountains

Written by Wim Coleman and Pat Perrin
Illustrated by Joanne Renaud

RED CHAIR
•PRESS•

Please visit our website at **www.redchairpress.com** for more high-quality products for young readers.

 EDUCATORS: Find FREE lesson plans and a Readers' Theater script for this book at www.redchairpress.com/free-activities.

About the Authors

Wim Coleman and Pat Perrin

Coleman and Perrin, a husband and wife writing team, have written over 100 publications. For 13 years these former teachers lived in San Miguel de Allende, Mexico where they created and managed a scholarship program for at-risk youth.

The Runaway Train: Saved by Belle of the Mines and Mountains

Publisher's Cataloging-In-Publication Data
(Prepared by The Donohue Group, Inc.)

Coleman, Wim.
   Runaway train : saved by Belle of the Mines and Mountains / written by Wim Coleman and Pat Perrin ; illustrated by Joanne Renaud.

   pages : illustrations ; cm. -- (Setting the stage for fluency)

   Summary: In 1856, 15-year-old Bella Lee Dunkinson began hanging around the local railroad in western Tennessee. Engineer John Hardiman took a liking to the spirited girl and gave her a boy's responsibilities helping with the engine. One stormy night, the engine was slipping dangerously on wet rails. While John was putting sand on the tracks, Bella found herself alone in the cab driving the train up a steep and dangerous mountainside. After her heroic and triumphant climb to the mountaintop, she was hailed by the miners who met her there as the "Belle of the Mines and Mountains."
   Interest age level: 009-012.
   Issued also as an ebook.
   Includes bibliographical references.
   ISBN: 978-1-939656-71-1 (library binding/hardcover)
   ISBN: 978-1-939656-72-8 (paperback)

   1. Dunkinson, Bella Lee--Juvenile drama. 2. Railroad engineers--Tennessee--Biography--Juvenile drama. 3. Railroad trains--Tennessee--History--Juvenile drama. 4. Dunkinson, Bella Lee--Drama. 5. Railroad engineers--Tennessee--Biography--Drama. 6. Railroad trains--Tennessee--History--Drama. 7. Children's plays, American. 8. Historical drama. 9. Biographical drama. I. Perrin, Pat. II. Renaud, Joanne. III. Title.

PS3553.O47448 R86 2015
(Fic)   2014944177

Copyright © 2015 Red Chair Press LLC

Photo on page 39: iStockphoto

This series first published by:
Red Chair Press LLC   PO Box 333   South Egremont, MA 01258-0333

Printed in the United States of America

1 2 3 4 5 18 17 16 15 14

TABLE OF CONTENTS

INTRODUCTION

This play is based on a true story titled "A Locomotive Engineeress," which appeared in the magazine *Frank Leslie's Popular Monthly* in 1888. It was written by an author named Bella Lee Dunkinson. The story tells of her adventure as a teenager many years earlier. Not long before the Civil War, Dunkinson and her family moved to the Cumberland Mountains in Western Tennessee. There she had a most unusual experience aboard a steam locomotive.

Dunkinson did not feel very welcome in Tennessee. She and her family had arrived there from a Northern state. Tennessee was a Southern state. When the Civil War broke out in 1861, Tennessee joined the Confederacy, the Southern states in rebellion against the Union. As a Northerner, Dunkinson found it difficult to make friends her age. She spent much of her time around steam locomotives. Engineers, the drivers of the locomotives, sometimes gave her work to do. This was unusual for a girl. In those days, girls and women had fewer opportunities for education and work than they do today.

Railroads spread through the Eastern United States in the early 1800s. During the Civil War, both the Union and Confederate armies used trains for military purposes. A transcontinental railroad linking the Pacific and Atlantic coasts was completed in 1869.

THE CAST OF CHARACTERS

Older Bella: Bella Lee Dunkinson as the narrator, in 1888, age 47

Younger Bella: age 15 in 1856 when story takes place

Father: Bella's father, about age 35

Teenagers 1, 2, and 3: females, about age 15

Mother: Bella's mother, about age 30

Arnold: the telegraph operator

John Hardiman: the train's engineer

Nelly Hardiman: John Hardiman's wife

Joe: the train's fireman

Pete: the train's conductor

Billy: the train's flagman

Coal miners 1, 2, 3, and 4

Coal miner's wife

Setting: Cowan's Station in Eastern Tennessee; aboard a train connecting Cowan's Station with a coal mine; a mining station high up in Cumberland Mountains.

Time: Narrated in 1888; the main story takes place in 1856.

PROLOGUE

Older Bella: Look what I just found upstairs. This pretty red coral necklace! It's been years since I've seen it. I'd almost forgotten I had it. I got it as a gift, some thirty-one or thirty-two years ago. The memories it brings back! Those men's voices as they raised their glasses, **toasting** me! I can hear them as if it were yesterday …

Miners: *(together, in Bella's memory)* To Bella Dunkinson, our **Belle** of the mines and mountains!

Older Bella: That's right, a "Belle." That's what they call a pretty young woman in the South—a "Southern Belle." Are you surprised? Me, Bella Lee Dunkinson, lady journalist of Boston, Massachusetts? A born-and-bred **Yankee**? But it's true, I was once called a Southern Belle. Let me tell you how it happened …

SCENE ONE

Older Bella: When I was growing up, my father worked for the Nashville & Chattanooga Railroad. He managed whole regions of the railroad—a "line officer," he was called. In 1856, he was put in charge of Cowan's Station in Tennessee. He and my mother and I moved there that year.

Father: *(in Bella's memory)* It's a fine job. The train here is very important. It moves supplies and coal to and from the Cumberland Mountain coal mines.

Older Bella: But the hills were a big change for me. I was fifteen years old. In the North I'd always lived in a big city. I'd gone to school and had lots of social activities. There had been tea parties, knitting circles, and dances. But there was no schooling for girls in that part of rural Tennessee. And as for making friends with other girls my age …

Teenager 1: Bella, you say your name is?

Teenager 2: The way you talk sounds odd.

Teenager 3: It's your accent. Where are you from?

Younger Bella: My family has lived in lots of places. Manhattan, Philadelphia, Boston …

Older Bella: The girls laughed …

Teenager 1: Oh, a Yankee girl!

Teenager 2: Bella—the "Northern Belle!"

Teenager 3: I didn't know there was such a thing.

Teenager 1: There's not. All "belles" come from the South.

Teenager 2: I'm afraid you just don't belong here, Bella.

Teenager 3: You and your family should just go home.

Older Bella: They were so mean to me. I asked my mother and father why …

Mother: I was afraid this would happen.

Father: I hoped it wouldn't be this bad.

Younger Bella: But what is it? What's wrong with me?

Mother: There's nothing wrong with *you*, Bella.

Father: Something's wrong with the whole country, though. The North and South are growing farther and farther apart. Southern slavery is the problem. There's talk of the Southern states seceding—breaking away from the Union.

Mother: And we're in the South now.

Father: There's even talk of a war.

Younger Bella: What would we do then?

Father: Move back North, I'm sure. Meanwhile, people here are not always going to be friendly.

Mother: And poor Bella! It's going to be so hard for you to make friends!

Father: Well, you're a bright, brave girl. You'll find some way to get along. Why don't you come down to the station with me tomorrow morning? The folks who work for me don't seem to mind having a Yankee around.

Older Bella: Early the next morning, Father and I drove to the train yard in our one-horse buggy. A train with only a few cars stood waiting at the station.

Younger Bella: Where is this train going, Father?

Father: It makes the daily trip up and down the mountain, to the mine and back.

Older Bella: As we walked past the little red caboose at the back, Father showed me the other cars.

Father: This open-topped car is called a gondola. On the way back from the mine, it will be loaded up with coal. These flat cars piled with wooden crates are full of supplies needed up at the mine. So are the box cars. Have you ever gotten a close look at a steam locomotive? It's quite a machine!

Older Bella: Just then a man wearing a green **visor** stepped out of the telegraph office.

Arnold: G'morning, Mr. Dunkinson.

Father: Good morning to you, Arnold.

Arnold: Sorry to trouble you, sir, but you've got an **urgent** message from the mine. They need a reply right soon.

Father: This might take a while, Bella. Why don't you wander around the yard? There's a lot to see, so look things over. Ask questions, too. The fellows here'll be glad to tell you whatever you want to know.

Older Bella: Father stepped into the office. I found myself standing beside the locomotive. I'd ridden lots of trains, but I'd never stood this close to a steam engine. I was in awe. It was so big and powerful. The two main wheels stood taller than I was. A stream of black smoke flowed upward from the huge, balloon-shaped smoke stack. A steady jet of white, hissing steam gushed out of the engine right in front of me. A man's voice called out …

Mr. Hardiman: Hullo there, young lady! May I help you?

Older Bella: A man was looking down at me from the cab. He was wearing thinly-striped overhauls and a puffy, thinly-striped cap.

Mr. Hardiman: My name's John Hardiman. I'm the engineer.

Younger Bella: My name's Bella.

Mr. Hardiman: Would you like a look inside?

Younger Bella: Oh, yes! Thanks!

Older Bella: Mr. Hardiman reached down and took my hand. He helped me up into the cab. It was full of gauges, cranks, sticks, and levers. Another man dressed like Mr. Hardiman was there.

Mr. Hardiman: This here's Joe Wilkinson, my fireman.

Joe: *(laughing)* Not the kind of fireman who puts out a burning house fire. My job's to keep this fire burning right.

Older Bella: Joe was carrying coal from the open car behind the locomotive and piling it into the roaring furnace.

Joe: The oil pressure might be getting a mite bit high. Would you have a look?

Older Bella: Mr. Hardiman peered closely at a clock-shaped gauge.

Mr. Hardiman: Pressure's two-fifteen, just like it should be. It's getting a little hard to read, though.

Older Bella: I could see why …

Younger Bella: Maybe I can help with that.

Older Bella: … so I pulled out my handkerchief and wiped the gauge's glass face. It had gotten awfully dirty.

Mr. Hardiman: That's better. Thanks. You're right helpful, young lady.

Joe: The other gauges are getting pretty **grimy**. The water glass too. I was fixing to wipe them off. Ran a bit short on time though.

Younger Bella: I could do that.

Mr. Hardiman: We'd appreciate it. But don't spoil that nice handkerchief. Here, this old rag is what we use.

Older Bella: I started wiping the other gauges. Then I heard Father's voice outside the cab.

Father: Hullo, Bella! Is that you up there?

Mr. Hardiman: You know this young 'un, Mr. Dunkinson?

Father: Why, she's my daughter! I see you've got her working, John.

Mr. Hardiman: Yes, sir, I suppose that's so.

Father: Well, Bella, you said just yesterday you needed something to do. Enjoying yourself, are you?

Younger Bella: I am, Father.

Older Bella: Father looked at his pocket watch.

Father: John, I see that you're pulling out of here in just a little while. Think you could keep her busy up the mountain and back?

Mr. Hardiman: I could at that.

Father: Well, take her along.

Mr. Hardiman: I will, sir. And I'll pay her too.

Father: Not too much. I don't want her spoiled. A penny for a day's work at most.

Older Bella: Father went on his way. I could hardly believe my good luck! I was so happy to have something to do!

Older Bella: I started wiping down everything that looked dirty. Right then a woman came along with a tray of steaming hot food.

Mrs. Hardiman: Good morning, fellows. Here's breakfast. But who's this?

Joe: Mr. Dunkinson just hired us a new hand.

Mr. Hardiman: Nelly, dear, meet Bella, Mr. Dunkinson's daughter. Bella, meet my wife, Nelly.

Younger Bella: Pleased to meet you, ma'am.

Mrs. Hardiman: Pleased to meet you too. The boss's daughter, eh? Well, I've always said this cab could use a woman's touch. I should have made breakfast for three. Should I fetch more food?

Younger Bella: No, thank you. I've had breakfast already.

Mrs. Hardiman: But goodness, child, you've already got a greasy spot on that pretty **linsey-woolsey** dress. That won't do. Let's go wash it right out. Come along with me.

Older Bella: I followed her to the neat little house where she and Mr. Hardiman lived. She lent me an overcoat …

Mrs. Hardiman: Put this on, it'll keep your dress from getting ruined. Have you got another dress you'd almost outgrown and were fixing to get rid of?

Younger Bella: I'm sure I do.

Mrs. Hardiman: Wear that tomorrow, then. You'll want these gloves, too. And things to clean with.

Older Bella: We loaded up a little wheelbarrow with everything we needed. A bucket, scrubbing brushes, and a bunch more old rags. Then we headed back to the train yard. We filled the bucket at the water pump and mixed in some lye. We scrubbed down everything in the cab, from the knobs, levers, and gauges down to the oak floor. It was eight-thirty by the time we'd finished—time to leave. Joe had **stoked** up the furnace, and the boiler was rumbling.

Mrs. Hardiman: You three have a good day. Bella, watch your step and do what you're told. You'll do just fine. John and Joe, you two watch your language. Or else I'll clean out somebody's mouth with this brush and lye water.

Older Bella: Mrs. Hardiman rolled the wheelbarrow away and headed back home. Joe sat down the left side of the cab and watched over the gauges. Mr. Hardiman took a seat on the right. He took hold of a big lever planted in the floor and pushed it forward.

Mr. Hardiman: Do me a favor, Bella, and pull that rope overhead.

Older Bella: I pulled the rope—and oh, what a noise! I almost jumped out of my skin! It was the train whistle. I'd heard lots of train whistles before, but never from inside a locomotive cab. How piercing it was! Joe and Mr. Hardiman laughed at my surprise. I laughed too.

Mr. Hardiman: You'd better take hold of something.

Older Bella: I grabbed the nearest post.

Mr. Hardiman: Now I'm releasing the brake.

Older Bella: Mr. Hardiman pulled a brass lever, and the locomotive suddenly **lurched**.

Mr. Hardiman: Now I'm pulling the throttle.

Older Bella: He pulled back a long handle hanging overhead.

Mr. Hardiman: Hold on tight now.

Older Bella: And it was a good thing I did. The engine jerked and halted, staggered and stopped, then staggered again. I could hear and feel all the cars behind us pushing and pulling and slamming each other. The engine let out a slow chug-chug-chugging sound. Little by little, the motion smoothed. The chug-chug-chugging grew faster. We moved along, slow and steady. The wheels on the tracks clattered and clacked. A thick **plume** of black smoke rolled along above and behind us. My heart thrilled as we picked up speed.

Mr. Hardiman: We're on our way!

Older Bella: I kept working for Mr. Hardiman, making a penny a day. I seldom thought about tea parties, knitting circles, or dances. Really, I felt a little sorry for girls who spent all their time that way. They had no idea how much fun they were missing! Mr. Hardiman found lots for me to do …

Mr. Hardiman: Bella, would you oil that **valve**?

Older Bella: I learned all about the locomotive, both inside and out …

Mr. Hardiman: The water glass tells you if the boiler's got too much water or too little.

Older Bella: He showed me how everything worked …

Mr. Hardiman: The brakes are powered by steam, just like everything else.

Older Bella: He even let me handle the controls once in a while …

Mr. Hardiman: The Johnson bar here makes 'er go forward or back. It also helps control speed. Handle it gently.

Older Bella: I suppose I learned as much about that locomotive as a male **apprentice** would …

Mr. Hardiman: The throttle controls how much steam goes into the engine.

Older Bella: But an apprentice would get to be an engineer himself someday …

Mr. Hardiman: Pay close attention to both the Johnson bar and the throttle.

Older Bella: I was never going to be an engineer—that was a *man's* job …

Mr. Hardiman: Always be watching your speed *and* your flow of steam.

Older Bella: I thought that was a shame …

Mr. Hardiman: You're smart and hard-working, Bella.

Older Bella: I think Mr. Hardiman thought so too.

Mr. Hardiman: You'd make a fine engineer someday.

Scene Six

Older Bella: I even went with Mr. Hardiman and Joe on night runs once or twice a week. It was raining one evening when I showed up for work.

Mr. Hardiman: Am I glad to see you, Bella! I was just over at Joe's house. He's awfully sick with a fever. So bad he can't get on his feet.

Younger Bella: He won't be coming?

Mr. Hardiman: No. It's a lot to ask, but do you think you can be my fireman this run?

Younger Bella: I'll try.

Older Bella: I started loading the firebox. Moving all that coal was heavier work than I was used to. But I'd gotten stronger working on the locomotive, and my hands had gotten tougher. I pulled the whistle when it came time to leave, and Mr. Hardiman took the controls. We were on our way.

Mr. Hardiman: I hope this rain doesn't give us much trouble.

Older Bella: But when we were ten minutes out, the drizzle turned into a fierce downpour. The noisiest thunderclap I'd ever heard shook the whole engine. Wind blew rain into the cab. We were soaked to the skin. We shouted to make ourselves heard.

Younger Bella: Should we stop?

Mr. Hardiman: Not on this slope. And we sure can't turn a freight train around on its tracks.

Older Bella: It was a twenty-five mile climb up that steep, winding mountain track. An ordinary run took an hour and ten minutes. But this wasn't going to be an ordinary run.

Mr. Hardiman: I've never seen a storm this bad. Give us more steam to beat this wind.

Younger Bella: How much coal do we need?

Mr. Hardiman: As much as you can manage!

Older Bella: Carrying coal from the fuel car, I felt like I was swimming against the downpour. I piled more and more coal into the firebox. The fire blazed so hot I could barely breathe. I thought I'd faint dead away. But I kept right on stoking the fire. After a while, Mr. Hardiman shouted out …

Mr. Hardiman: Stop a minute there, Bella. Look at that boiler gauge. She can't take more steam. It's all she can stand. Don't want this machine to explode!

Older Bella: I shouted at the top of my lungs to make myself heard …

Younger Bella: What do I do now?

Older Bella: He didn't answer. He was staring outside. By the light of the swinging cab lantern, I glimpsed terror in his eyes.

Mr. Hardiman: Hang it all, I can't even tell where we are!

Older Bella: I stepped dizzily over to my own front window.

Younger Bella: I can't see ahead either! Has the forward lamp gone out?

Mr. Hardiman: I don't guess so. Rain's coming down too thick for the light to cut through. See anything to your left?

Younger Bella: Not a thing! It's pitch dark all over.

Mr. Hardiman: We're running blind.

Older Bella: Just then came a flash of lightning. As the thunder roared, I glimpsed the surrounding forest …

Younger Bella: Oh, no!

Mr. Hardiman: What is it?

Younger Bella: We're standing still!

Mr. Hardiman: Just as I feared.

Younger Bella: But how? The engine's going full throttle!

Mr. Hardiman: Wheels are spinning on the tracks. We're wasting steam. Water too.

Older Bella: He pulled back the throttle lever. The chug-chug-chugging slowed down and nearly stopped.

Younger Bella: Should I put on the brakes?

Mr. Hardiman: Got to. They won't hold long, though.

Older Bella: He grabbed a heavy bucket.

Mr. Hardiman: Got to put sand under the wheels.

Younger Bella: I'll go do it.

Mr. Hardiman: No you won't. Once we get moving again, there won't be any stopping. I can't risk leaving you alone in this storm.

Younger Bella: But one of us has got to run the train!

Older Bella: He patted me on the shoulder.

Mr. Hardiman: It's got to be you!

Older Bella: He jumped down off the engine.

SCENE SEVEN

Older Bella: I was more frightened than I'd been in my life.

Younger Bella: *Can* I do it?

Older Bella: I checked the water glass.

Younger Bella: Oh, no!

Older Bella: The level was low.

Younger Bella: We've used too much water!

Older Bella: I wasn't sure the locomotive could finish the trip.

Younger Bella: Mr. Hardiman! Can you hear me?

Older Bella: But I could barely hear my own voice.

Younger Bella: Where is he?

Older Bella: I peered outside through flashes of lightning.

Younger Bella: Mr. Hardiman!

Older Bella: I glimpsed him making his way around the engine, scattering sand as he went. Then came a terrifying lurch.

Younger Bella: She's sliding backwards!

Older Bella: If I didn't do something, there'd be no stopping the downhill slide.

Younger Bella: The brakes will give! She'll fly off the tracks! And the mountainside is **sheer**!

Older Bella: I hoped Mr. Hardiman had put down enough sand. The rest was up to me. I told myself what to do.

Younger Bella: Release the brake …

Older Bella: I did, and the train rolled backward faster.

Younger Bella: *(to self)* Now pull the throttle … carefully, oh so carefully.

Older Bella: Too much steam and the wheels would spin again. The chug-chug-chugging of the engine picked up. The locomotive stopped still for a second or two. And then …

Younger Bella: She's moving forward!

Older Bella: I called outside …

Younger Bella: Mr. Hardiman! It worked! The sand worked!

Older Bella: I heard his voice slipping behind into the dark storm …

Mr. Hardiman: More steam!

Older Bella: I pushed the throttle again. The locomotive now **hurtled** along. Then came the hard part …

Younger Bella: She's rounding a curve.

Older Bella: She was picking up too much speed.

Younger Bella: She'll run right off the mountainside!

Older Bella: I remembered my lessons …

Younger Bella: Control the steam *and* the speed …

Older Bella: I took hold of both the throttle and the Johnson bar …

Younger Bella: Slow down for the curve … pick up speed for the straight climb …

Older Bella: I still couldn't see a thing. But I guided the controls perfectly. I kept the train on the rails, curve after curve. I looked at the water glass …

Younger Bella: Almost empty!

Older Bella: And the steam gauge was falling.

Younger Bella: Not enough steam!

Older Bella: I could feel the engine weakening.

Younger Bella: The slope is still so steep!

Older Bella: The chug-chug-chugging came slower and softer.

Younger Bella: I'll never make the summit!

Older Bella: But just then, the slope leveled out. I looked outside.

Younger Bella: There it is! Light from the mine!

Older Bella: The train rolled up to the platform and came to a stop. At that very moment, the chug-chug-chugging ended. All the steam was gone. I'd made the climb up the mountain—but only just barely!

EPILOGUE

Older Bella: I saw a hundred little lights gathering around the locomotive.

Younger Bella: The miners … the gas lamps on their hats.

Miner 1: Hullo there, Hardiman!

Miner 2: We thought you were a goner in this rain!

Miner 3: We'd given up hope!

Miner 4: Well done, well done!

Older Bella: But then one of them looked into the cab …

Miner 1: Why, it's only young Bella!

Miner 2: Where's John Hardiman?

Older Bella: I was wet and shaking from the cold—and also from fear and relief. I climbed down from the cab and told them as well as I could what had happened.

Younger Bella: He's back yonder on the tracks. Somebody needs to go get him.

Older Bella: The storm was dying down by then. A couple of men took a hand car down the slope and fetched Mr. Hardiman. He was wet and cold too, but safe and sound. The miners gave us fresh, dry clothes and a fire to warm ourselves. One of their wives gave me this necklace …

Miner's Wife: You've earned it, young lady! You saved the train—and both of your lives besides!

Older Bella: She also gave me a welcome cup of hot coffee. The men poured glasses of whiskey all around. Mr. Hardiman raised his glass.

Mr. Hardiman: Gentlemen, I'd like to make a toast. To Bella Dunkinson, our Belle of the mines and mountains!

Miners: *(together)* To Bella Dunkinson, our Belle of the mines and mountains!

Older Bella: And that's how I became a true Southern Belle!

WORDS TO KNOW

apprentice: a person who is learning a trade from a skilled worker

belle: a very popular and attractive girl or woman

grimy: covered with grime, dirt smeared on a surface

hurtled: rushed ahead wildly at great speed

lurch: a sudden sideways movement

plume: a long cloud of smoke shaped like a feather

sheer: vertical, steep

stoke: add fuel to a furnace

toast: to drink in honor of someone

urgent: important, needing immediate attention

visor: a stiff brim on a hat that shades the eyes

Yankee: a person from New England or another Northern state

linsey-woolsey: a strong fabric made of wool and either cotton or linen.

valve: a thing to control the passage of fluid

Learn More About the Rails and Mining

Books:

Hodge, Deborah. *The Kids Book of Canada's Railway: And How the CPR Was Built*. Kids Can Press, 2010.

Perritano, John. *The Transcontinental Railroad* (True Books). Scholastic, 2010.

Web Sites:

Tennessee's rich mining history:
http://www.tnhistoryforkids.org/geography/a_6

Dunlap Coke Mines history:
http://www.tnhistoryforkids.org/places/dunlap_museum

Places:

Dunlap Coke Mines history:
Museum & Park: Dunlap, TN

Narrow Gauge Railroad Museum:
Located in an 1882 depot, Durango, CO.

Ride the coal-fired steam locomotive from Durango to Silverton, CO.